THE LEAST IMPORTANT MAN

the least important man

alex boyd

poems

BIBLIOASIS

FIRST EDITION

Library and Archives Canada Cataloguing in Publication

Boyd, Alex, 1969-
    The least important man / Alex Boyd.

Poems.
ISBN 978-1-926845-40-1

    I. Title.

PS8603.O98L42 2012   C811'.6   C2011-907869-4

 Canada Council   Conseil des Arts
for the Arts   du Canada

 Canadian   Patrimoine
Heritage   canadien

 ONTARIO ARTS COUNCIL
CONSEIL DES ARTS DE L'ONTARIO

Biblioasis acknowledges the ongoing financial support of the Government of Canada through the Canada Council for the Arts, Canadian Heritage, the Canada Book Fund; and the Government of Ontario through the Ontario Arts Council.

PRINTED AND BOUND IN CANADA

Contents

THE LEAST IMPORTANT MAN

The Least Important Man

It's a smaller jar or worry and keys in his bag,
but he's busy: riding streetcars, making hidden
gestures that prevent accidents all around, at work
typing for tight-lipped old Danish twins, wide-eyed
as owls and alarmed at an unplanned paper clip.
Monday morning they start to step up to his counter,
and in offices everywhere, the public signs the world
into existence. Signatures that look like a mailbox,
a bullwhip, you with two portions humping, you
with fish hooks in air, the bent heart in soup,
swing set and breeze, lion in the grass of a last name,
and you, the perfect schoolteacher as model.

You missed him. He's down the hall, behind the door
with better ideas, arranging attraction in old magnets,
or on a sojourn for benevolence, undulating on the ocean,
leaving antiquated opinions on a Paris café counter
about a lack of agony, revenge as a sloppy virus.
No one notices his ears are paler, two alert ghosts
on his head, or his fondness for buying frames.
He writes postcards about spring cracking open the land
with an edge tight as a bowstring: a man running
is shocking - he looks refracted like a stick in water,
that he is not head bent under cutting winds. And,
strange to be outside watching, framed between
the blue and growing green, smiling from a bench
thinking of the kiss he pushed under sheets
to her cheek, a smile sprouting beneath closed eyes.

He'll work on it, when he thinks there's some point
to trying, wallpapers small rooms with his best images.
He'll think along other voices, a bird on a phone line,

scoop up what we miss under speech, try to steal
away softly as a cat under the glow of a window.
But he's making changes, tired of writing notes
that already don't matter – he'll find new work,
he'll sacrifice his stomach, will never last
long enough to be an old man, slowly navigating
his pale, dented ass into a seat on the subway.

The guy at the video store was always a trifle nervous,
but now there's no eye contact at all, he punches
up titles, stabs buttons with cuts on his hands,
no longer shares video wisdom but lectures, so
the least important man tells him off, tears over
to the grocery store in his shiny new jeep – you'd think
he could unhook bones, the way he slips by displays,
drops overpriced pine nuts so quickly, others
watching must believe he'd make a fine sniper.
And then he's gone, having taken nine items
through the one-to-eight line, waved a finger lightly
at peanut butter, saying *I'll be back for you, fucker.*
Because what is he told, but that he should practice
being someone else, someone else?

A Glimpse of My Bright Life in the Morning

I catch a glimpse of my bright life in the morning,
before I begin, it looks like a small dog
up at me to ask which way to go, as I bend
to put on shoes. I step on it for the first
time that day going out the door, then it sees
where we're going, to the office to know
only certain kinds of corners, sharp metal gods
the size of filing cabinets, each day a bundle
of time dropped like a newspaper on my step
and layered so similarly, down to the mall at lunch
(garbage can, bench, plant, bench, garbage can).
I see a man caught in the eye of a camera.
He watches himself on TV, raises an arm,
at last reflected in the face that means so much.
Somehow sad, wrapped in the flag of a trench coat.
I look back, see he's still caught in the spell,
step out to get the brochure reminder: except a man
be born again, he cannot see the kingdom of God.
And the man who misses the garbage, keeps going
takes one small piece of my hope, but I get it back
from the crooked wave of a co-worker I like.
At home I get in the door, catch another look
as my life reappears, and like a wet dog
shakes itself off. Covered in pins, useless notes,
it looks up at me again. I'm tired, I say.

1977

Start of the year I was seven, told in a hardware store you don't
buy a pile of corks for nothing – but they were impressive,
so I stuffed handfuls down my snowsuit, not thinking ahead
to my mother helping me out of it, unzipping the front and
all the corks popping out everywhere. She pretended to be
angry, wagged her finger at me, my father returned with a
brown paper bag full of corks. In the summer I turned eight,
Star Wars was the coolest, and the *Enterprise* took a test flight,
clinging to a 747.

The word *building* is always in the present tense, never finished.
Summers, they go up slowly, fattening skeletons, groping
to sky, cranes nodding promises and forgetting. The Silver
Jubilee of Queen Elizabeth II meant lining up at school, out
in the heat, handed a cheap coin I cherished, my loyalty so
absolute I took it straight home to put it somewhere so safe it
was outside of the world – lost. On August 16, Elvis died. A
kid said he was glad, and I thought *you're too young to have an
opinion like that.*

September, Voyager 1 launched to slide Saturn's rings, stare
Jupiter in the eye, and now a hundred times further from the
sun than earth, looks back and winks each day. Impressive as
it is, it's still like standing at the edge of the largest parking lot
you can imagine and rolling a dime into it – a million miles a
day and still forty thousand years from another solar system.
Voyager 2 left a month earlier, but will never pass it, thanks to
angles, gravity slingshots, and I'll never completely understand
that, gripping my glass, the world spinning at a thousand miles
an hour.

To a Businessman at Rush Hour

You can't even make a decent fucking sword,
and it's a fat briefcase you jam between doors
to get on board, grey manta ray coat flapping.
The world was made for businessmen, the rest
of us just live here. They saunter down
the middle of grocery aisles, wanting,
come swarming boneless out of cracks (jerking
at stuck briefcases) like roaches, even where
people have sprayed to have them kept at bay –
the painter wanting his studio to himself,
turning to find a businessman lying bloated
and unhappy in the centre of the room, whispering
orders for another mountain to be levelled.

The Balding Man Feels the Music

A large crown of skin on top of his head,
he reaches up into air for handfuls of nothing.
This place bulges with drum, fiddle and pipes
that drill at least an inch into the walls.
Now the arm comes up a little, back and forth
just above waist level, he's marching
fixed and alone at his two-person table.
Crawls through a job he hates all week
towards weekends flagged in colour, waving.
Suddenly in the thick of the music he's up,
tipping tables and lifting chairs, checking
around for something, and for an instant
opens his arms and stands looking at me,
lost expression over the fifty-something face.
Then someone kindly hands him the rattle
I never saw in his hand, or flying from it
and he's once more elected at his table,
the marching leader of a tiny, perfect country.

Canada Day Snapshot, 2004

I'm a part of Canada, maybe a corpuscle
doing laundry, noting the constant position
of the homeless man, laundromat rambler,
standing rigidly on guard, looking out the window
saying *got no tools slap the bitch,* and so on
before he walks over to politely ask, *Excuse me,*
do you have the time? as though he takes fifteen-
minute breaks, goes back to having an exposed heart
like a plum on the sidewalk. Out there, streetcars,
a red and white blur of steel, grumbling
and hushing, giving birth to people all the way
down the street, tucked into the effort of their lives,
the difficult bloodstream of a proud nation.
Down the street I smile at a bald man in a window
putting soup into his potato face, fire trucks with
boots in overalls squatting on each side as though
firefighters dissolved. Another piece of Canada
close to home, in the shape of an old woman
on her way to Chinatown, arms around groceries,
a tiny receipt flutters in her hand, celebrating wildly.

Someday the Men with Hats Will Go

Someday all the old men in hats will go,
they already slow motion down streetcar steps
the forties, cigarettes, black and white wars
swimming behind them. They line up patiently
to get last passports in offices, wait behind youth.
They take receipts, pause to leak out the words
All the best to you, and step into oblivion.
I look for something different all the way home.
The snow is tired, deep in contours of the brain,
finally now evaporating to liquid, so much theft
a natural part of the world – the fact that I have
my father's eyes, my body the next edition,
walking the earth in different places, impure
from smoke that went from his lungs to mine
before he quit in 1977, another detail I wrote
down after another dinner with him. This spring
my father will be seventy-four, yet another step
higher on the ladder and I cannot tell you
how much I'm afraid of that red day, unlike
any other, when I'll sail along rails alone,
when he evaporates, when both of them
will be gone, my voice or ankle part of a model
with no origin, the factory now demolished.
What will be left, but some kind of liquid dream,
the hope of knowing a father again, the two of us
back as birches. No more distances, I want
many long thin fingers in winter, holding his.

And the Morning Brings Rush Hour

As though we all prayed through the night:
let me apologize to strangers, press me near
small mustached men in huge headphones
blinking time away, old men who sip
coffee into a thin frames, have a medical
emergency on the train, announcements
about delays. A man terribly conscious of being
close to forty hopes he'll be able to concentrate
on his empty little paper datebook as a way
to avoid really seeing the ex across from him,
maybe getting frustrated enough to say
speak to me, or ignore me, but quit staring
at me from behind the damn sunglasses.
Two others want to meet, their cars kissing
black and olive shards of plastic and glass,
and oh, to shake hands with a kind stranger,
by this tiny new landscape on the road.
A woman hopes to tie her shoelace, crouched
while dozens pass funhouse reflections,
fluttering silver doors saying *just go, just go.*
She gets to work to draw a wavy heartbeat line
that much farther through a calendar on the wall.

Two Thirteen-Line Poems on How
We Need a New Poem

But only a good one. Hammer, mine the day.
Have other poems dropped like depth charges
to break something loose, picture a tight-lipped
brigadier, reciting a roll call, "Acorn, Akhmatova"
loaded – fired against the circle of whiteness
surrounding the city – reload – and again.
And old women, helping the effort, walk
the streets beating pans to flush out a poem,
report that an old Chinese man looked into
Wah Fook Seafood Trading and smiled, lifted
the stick of an arm and waved gently like a king.
I need something more, comes the reply, more than
police cruisers sailing the streets like sharks.

The young man on the street corner is always there,
growing the thin film of hostility on the inside
of his frame, that much extra weight in a bucket –
heart stamping each day like a blown tire,
not speaking because he knows his voice would sound
like an angry dog – his pet rats lined up on his arm,
even seem frightened, as though on a sinking ship,
the sign reading *out of work out of home please*
help thank you, nobody from the passing
stream stops to think if he were God, quietly there,
even a dollar would get you into heaven.
He knows, instead, the fussing crow wing
of a broken umbrella, waving him away.

Formula for the Body
and the Bullet

1.
The body is more than the bullet.
The brain sends out signals and for now,
let's call this a courier – handsome
young galloping lad. Without tired,
how would bones know they rest in muscle,
a herd of bulls waiting for orders?
Blood is shy, all day hiding in you
and asking the same worried questions.
The things that the mind learns
while it hangs on a thread
(the Chinese character for sound
combines SUN and RISE for when
the world wakes with the light
and sounds of life begin).

2.
The bullet is less than the body,
simpler. Gunpowder and a small,
metal exclamation mark.
The bullet can end the body.
The bullet makes the news.
Money, in an alley, listens and plans –
it knows better than us what fears
we pass from one mind to the next,
through the generations.

3.
The body builds more bullets, and
we go back to step one.

How Words Feel

There are long stages where the things you have to show
for your time on the earth are rudimentary skills:
a hot plate and locusts, a knife and fork. Or sleeplessness,
the salacious stories creeping over the wide cake of dirt
and grass to pour slowly in through the basement window.
Words lie quiet in lines: flat as a road map, winsome-faced,
and planning, a pleasant battalion. You put your hand in them,
and feel around – curious – finding polished ideas, fossils
frozen while stepping, snail of a comma. Tossing them lightly
gives you the weight, an emergent prod like an egg hatching.
A *Tale of Two Cities* dies in my hands and pages drop like leaves,
wanting to hum all night under the bed about brotherhood, salient
bonds. I can think of worse things to escort me through dreams,
a piece of brown cover coming off, found on my black t-shirt,
like a raft at night. The name Bob Holloway, his drawing of a girl,
crooked smile and pencil-curly hair on thin, browning paper.

Captain Kirk Love Poem

There was some small moment at the start, wasn't there,
some touch: the most dazzelous woman you'd ever seen,
there on a street corner and you left, made excuses
like she's on a bike, I've got to get this package home.
It was before you knew your body swarmed with luck,
a black and gold uniform of mashed black-eyed Susans
and lurking, tamed mustard gas reinforcing your eyes.
You thought to make up for it: time travel slingshots,
cacophony of rankled emperors, altered comets, viruses
and wicked computers trashed, your scattered children.
You charmed the tall freckled women of Widow Avenue,
and were gone, never seen on a doddering bus to have
some old woman's purse full of tissues and lozenges
kiss your knee and carry on. But there was a whisper.
A worry the further you went, the more you missed, some
combination of null space. Back there, a former self aghast
to face that we're weak and beautiful, made of sticks,
honey, water and ranunculi holding up under the wind,
or that one place is shiny with multitudes, if you stay
long enough to see it. Or that we can be manta ray thin,
but blue whale big-hearted. We needed you, can note
your example, splendour-addicted, finally seeing the woman
who reminds you most of her, and disappearing
in your own pattern: her green and black floral dress,
the thin river of a burst of sun standing up, as if to speak.

Rod Serling's Funeral, 1975

It's either a bulldog or bullet ant, lovingly
transported, expected to go unnoticed
in the particular shadows of the asphalt.
Up above, the gargoyle has flashbacks
to World War Two, even as a crane lands
on a tarp over the door. Someone entering
comments, *he was the son of a butcher,*
but would never have hurt that bird.
Inside, a series of photos, beginning
with a camera whirl, and Serling with a smoke
steps out from the bushes, monochromatic,
to explain a beginning, a restrained blackness
in the suit. In the crowded room, someone
nearly knocks one photo over, and a pocket
of old ladies hoot like owls. The one child
has disturbing eyes, pulls a string
and her doll asks *Mama, will I ever win?*
In a corner, a young man first hears of sushi,
comes up with a sharp, awkward metaphor
involving the rings of Saturn. It was season
one, 1959. And then everything changed,
another camera whirl, strong as an embrace.

Brick and Bone

Houses at night know fear, know barking dogs.
know the irregular orbit of cats, begin
the creak and settle, a kind of whale song,

swim quietly in formation, each window an eye,
feel the wide darkness as if it were water.
Houses know all kinds of dignity,

wait for old men to lie on park benches
like lizards in a rectangle of sun,
watch old women sweep the walk for hours.

They watch, more slowly, the change of leaves.
The Code for houses has been to know that brick
is stronger than bone – but worth far less.

Even a ghost, the echo of bone in rafters better
than nothing, than a hollow space,
when the glow of light and movement is like blood.

The Culture of Shyness

Sacraments of ducked heads and disappearances,

never interrupting a moment with a mobile phone,

renting videos unscathed, evenings dented

by someone's failure to respond, anxious

about asking for salt, unable to eat with someone

looking, arranging books and chairs in cafeterias

to create tents of space, floating in the babble,

making note of the spaces between steps, moments

between events, scattered human anchors

settled into the soil of peace and quiet to consider

progress. Stamped out by drama teachers.

Notes on a Small World

No part of either army mourns, refuses to move
for political reasons. Field clear and level,
each pawn moves straight. Forward, armed
with a spade, that's all. The bishop is cruelest.
Nobody knows why he asks to be served
those he slays with chutney. Nobody knows
he dreams of being handed his own severed head.
The knight has an odd but loyal compass, puts up
with the rook, his raucous affairs in the off-hours,
so frequently heard by the king, part dragon
but shifty and slow out of need to feel his aromatic
movement in silk. It's all about breeding, instinct.
There's no difference in resources between armies.
Reincarnation is a fact, but they get only one try
at this before beginning again. It is the queen who
works hardest, pregnant only with celestial concerns,
lands with both feet on an opponent, thinks ahead
to a summer of peace and freedom: a straw hat,
yellow dress. Little does she know, it's game over.

Remembrance Day, 2001

The potential hero across from me plays impatiently
with his newspaper transfer and my leather boots
take me the few steps from the streetcar to work.

Found a chap with my name on a monument once,
in Scotland, stood and touched the small letters.

The poppy a splash of blood on my shoulder
as my boots move through leaves, school-bus yellow
and the shhh as someone walks through leaves
matching the shhh of air as shells arrive for skulls.

Would it matter if anyone wrote a letter saying
killing Afghan children won't bring anyone back?

In a drizzle of rain, on a break from work
I read the final pages of Vimy, where five thousand
young Canadians die, turn the last brown page,
dry as an old leaf, read it was *a terrible waste*
of human life, brought on by greedy people
and tolerated for too long by silent majorities,
and my leather boots turn on gravel, back to work.

Undersea

I see her, working at the snack bar
held by long wooden fingers,
wriggling like something caught,
bent to clean mouse shit.
Standing under the angry Swedish man
who says *what's your name anyway*
one finger jigging over the counter,
trying to pin something. Behind her,
turn the tap on quickly and the water
leaps - a bird wanting the walls, anything.

I know her, she lowers her head under
a line of people passing as if they were
a wave of water, lifts her eyes again.
Her lover kisses her, not wanting her cold,
blows air like smoke each time, her eyes
calmly blinking it into bite-sized pieces.
Morning, coffee held against winter,
from her window she sees children climb
a park hill, sun on snow, small and wrapped
as astronauts on a bright new world.

Homage to Everything

You're a clever conceit, walking streets firmly believing
in yourself – relying on all that can fit on optic nerves,
like two hundred men fighting for rowboats. A waitress
nods, as if to acknowledge your fraction of lizard DNA.
And it's you that notes your wolverine hands at dinner,
extended by silver, a shining fork and knife after the food.
This is for you, and for the time-crippled old gentleman
who was never on that plane, and so survived to stand
in the corner of my eye a second. And for chenille plants,
foxtailed and falling outward like drunks on corners.

Guess what. God comes through that kind of humility –
the kind that's convinced cement will do as a kind of pillow
in a pinch. Look, he admits, you're more complicated
than me: relaxed cottager, Victorian leader, and sleeping lion
all engaged in a cultural cringe and baked together,
hiding under a plain crust, the echo of every taunt there
in the back of the mind. He looks at our odd clockwork –
not getting it right but we might – looks at the flexible billions,
puts a small blessing in each ramekin, smoothes down
a cyclone the way you would a cat, goes out the door again.

In Place

I can picture those who work in some way
to maintain me, like a pit crew, each insensible
to the rest: doctor, dentist, the lordly teens
who ring through my groceries so that they
drop the actions and me off the pier
of their memory, even as their arms move.
And for what, so I can work my own job,
greet a friend, see a film and emerge from darkness
to lift the tent pegs of my shoulders in a shrug.
Of anything, greeting a friend seems purest,
to live as scaffolding to one you admire.
My data entry and life in fear of suitcases
and lawyers could only work knowing I swim
vaguely towards some experience I'll enjoy,
raising a glass in a bar, and all of us aware
what part of us would have to fall away
for the system of support to do the same.
Beautifully, it has nothing to do with tonight,
the old lady by the door manipulating
her weight to get it open, whole body bent
like a bracket, some lesser thing to be said.

First World Wars

Summer and stepping outside to a wall of wood
lifting, I asked my father and grandfather what
they were doing – *building you a clubhouse* Dad said
grudgingly, as if I had demanded one (and now,
remembering the sound of hammers at work,
it felt like strange thunder, a warning).
We still have my grandfather's letters up to the end
of the war, 1918, and some give details: *the big shell
right in front of us that failed to explode. Lucky.*
Word spread to other houses, and near one
a wooden castle appeared in response, all the boys
of the street springing to one side or the other.
When my Dad was young my grandfather drank
and talked about turning a trench corner to come
face to face with one of them. *What did you do?*
I got my bayonet up first. I fought the other leader
and we fell through bushes without a scratch.
Sharpened popsicle sticks a purpose turned inside out,
plans for turning batteries into bombs stolen. Someone
defected to our side for a day. One morning, plaster
in my clubhouse lock. I cut an enemy lip, took a
blunt speech from his mother. And the tension, dull
electric, and constant. Boys charged from the bushes,
pushing one long sharpened branch. I fumbled keys
to get inside. Lucky. My grandfather noted an accident
in a letter: ironically, an electrocution days after the war.
He said *I guess they don't need a war to kill a man.*

Dream

It was something about a man, his long face
and uniform snapped orders, and friends were there,
defiant. We outnumbered him but walked around
where he was made of the same stuff as the arena.
He kept us from something – we couldn't tell what.
I even woke, then dropped back to sleep wanting
the next episode, knowing it would be wiped
clean as a blackboard. Finally, in the afternoon
drinking coffee, drawing the blinds to let Sunday
arrive in strips, sunlight stabbing – *you neglected me.*

We find dreams one at a time, assuming they happen
in fragments – but what if we learned to pound
and shape our dreams, to visit the same world
where it all unfolded, where the rich have a corner
to make unlimited money at no one's expense, where
I leap buildings to you, a crashing cyclist wipes
himself like eraser fragments from the scene to start again,
where you find a red scarf in a drizzle of rain,
pick up the owner and all her good ideas.
The truth is you use your dreams, or they use you.

Dead Bees Are Indomitable

Dead bees aren't seditious, they simply fly
with vague purpose, wear suits made of rain,
whatever else is all around them – they've
got fingerprints on you, put you in their last
will and testament, make their own music
as a way to tell themselves it's all right.
They ride the backs of living bees to reassure,
saying *whoops* when they bump something, or
when a living bee is snapped up by a bird, it's
a chipper *that didn't work out now did it?*
They still sense currents of air, citrus giving
them Jell-O legs for a moment, a short fever.
They're still fuzzy, but don't carry the electrostatic
charge to collect pollen. They look for summits
and connections, dazzled that as you slapped down
your newspaper, a car exploded in Paraguay.
They're sometimes knocked insensate by it all,
and can be found on your shoulder, recovering.
If we were to kill all these tidy little butlers,
we'd follow them, see the swarm like fuzz
on a TV set, and beg them to take a shape, please.

Vesta Lunch
2 A.M.

Rob and I sit on a stool
face the two old Italian men
sliding up and down
cutting through tasks like air,
tossing bread into toasters.
They could do anything.

     That man chopping food
     makes me happy, Rob says.

Somewhere in me a barrier breaks,
and I stop worrying about fights
(have I ever really been in one?)

and relax. Two omelettes already,
every back to the window.

The man further down says
he is worried about something –
I don't hear the quiet answer
coming from the cook.

Not every fortress
has high walls, I keep thinking.

     We pay down at the end?
He shrugs, yeah

While we stand there this man,
(who has no bruises but looks beaten)
the same man who has been bouncing

his voice off the two patient owners,
borrowing from them to buy
cigarettes, takes one now

stuffs it in my pocket
saying
          for good luck, for luck

the world breaking off
at the door

Eyes Only Know How to Steal

The eyes have it – it's all in those twins, a moon
and reflection at the forefront of things, first
to stab at the mist up ahead, like a crow's nest
for the human body. I'll tell you a secret:
I hate to be stared at more than anything, don't
know why it gives me that being-filmed feeling,
like being squeezed, as though everything seen is
scooped up, threaded through some invisible
process and at the moment of death, downloaded.
I want my eyes to have lasers – scorching corners
so others duck back, their ambition cut short.
Why I feel they're taking from me I'll never know –
we only go back to ourselves, as though to a well.

Now that my own sight finally threatens to blur, just
at the edges, sputter and fail, now that an eyebrow
isn't quite the same platoon, one insisting
on a solid grey uniform, another straying, I think
of my mother's eyes that saw me raised, now gone
like rotten eggs, years at the bottom of the fridge.
The idea that something can go out like a light,
after staring daggers, taking an expanse of mountains,
noting a smear campaign. Knowing they'll be vacated,
eyes only know how to steal. People see a photo
of my mother when young, her dark eyes and eyebrows
and I see odd meanings in that old expression
they say, unthinking: you have your mother's eyes.

The Weight of a Fool

The fool struck suddenly, like a meteor,
filled the air with broken earth. Late at night
on a quiet street the fool sang,
a fool imitation of the Chinese language,
after my friend as we pass and every window
shattered – a match of anger lit in my brain
but my throat only hissed the word *asshole*.
I leaked hate. All the kindness of a friend buried,
and when the dirt first hits your back and neck,
you think it's a shovelful but it's truckloads,
the world descending on itself, a new layer
of darkness, thick as a sack, taking the shape
of night, of everything: crickets, their music too.

Firenze

Cathedral bells built this poem.
The pepper of birds on an iron
grey sky over the red rooftops of Firenze.
With each bell a word rolled in.

The bells found everything:
us in the Boboli gardens under rain,
looking away from the roofs now
at the rusted handrail, and below that
the woman on the stone steps
beneath a red umbrella.

We stood an hour for Michelangelo,
but there is no lineup for gardens
in the rain, and there was none
for the old Italian man who washed
something small in the fountain.

No decision, easy to stop here
watch my love walk slowly away,
a yellow raincoat on black pants.

Elementary

You came from peace: a flat indigo sea, a cedar boat.
And you were born into the bustle and fuss of a hospital,
with people being paged to be where they aren't,
possible trails just beginning to become visible.
Just before you move out, returning home drunk,
stop at the public school where you were spanked
for laughing and piss on it long minutes, wonder
what devices were dropped into your mind, invisible
as something baked into a pie. Youth is a spray
of movement, denim-covered, raven-black hair.
You must learn to be completely at home in your skin.
Next are the afternoons in a small apartment filled
with heat: even a fly can mock you, landing
on your rolled-up newspaper, hope folded back like wings.

Things disappear under the cold water of forgetting,
and our salmon hearts won't stay forever, so I've saved
leptons and quarks from a handshake, will use them
to take something with me: George square in Glasgow,
where a red man says to stop, a green man says to go,
cabs black as beetles pass red lumbering buses, a man bolts,
an old lady hops a puddle, pigeons dip around your head.
I'll take the image of a woman lying back on a picnic,
smiling, dripping in sunlight that looks hard as apples.
When you're sick, you go to the bustle and fuss
of a hospital, hear people paged to be where they aren't,
and then back to peace: a flat indigo sea, a cedar boat.
At the moment all that you are showers out of you,
it will be so amazing that no one will be able to see it.

Summit

This isn't the light we wanted, the weather
we're supposed to be having. But it's still
sometimes all we have to talk about. We
put all our little fingertips in the sky
and changed the climate – those are your
fingerprints on the moon, and mine. Now
we've made room for these leaders,
appointments moving like flocks of birds
down the calendar. The police get sweeping
new powers to sweep us away, and we hope
this particular patchwork of leaders will give
a little thought to the little people, some
blank-eyed woman behind a window holding
a sandwich to her face like gauze to a wound.
Not to worry, there are key initiatives,
discussions. I know change, it's like a coin
we take out and toss again and again. All
we're doing is hanging like a water droplet.

Around One: Late Friday Subway Notes

Hands in your pockets you're frozen
in a tight shape, a constant lurch
and your hat a broken cake, the brim
first, then the fireworks of your hair,
the rest of it leaning away
from the perfect peace of your face
held just below a view of rushing.
But wrapped in thin dreams you race blissful
down the cold spine of the city
just the small rise and fall of your chest.

I saw the bubble of peace, the shell
protecting you. Fragile, destined
to be lost – you may not even remember
it after you wake and sink back into
what plagues you – your web of knowing.
But not yet, not yet, wait
while I come home to fold these words
into a silent paper boat.

The Dignity Machine

It hangs in the air five feet behind each of us,
needing fuel, clanking like an old film projector.
It hands you small memories unconsciously:
cold metal fire engine or muppet from childhood,
whatever gets you a step closer to a feeling,
some small heaven, a bridge to being ensconced
with a lover, salivating over the ticket of food.
The machine slows, squirrelly with tucked-away
pockets of bitterness. It cranks up, before flaming out
behind every gentle cow, runs on empty over the militia
as they march and wheel, opium minds set to loaf.
Even the carpenter ants in my bathroom know of it,
near starvation but sending out mad scouts, over
a landscape of broken tiles, tiny dignity machines
churning behind them, all wanting the same great
elusive accident of happiness, despite a slow truth,
our elfin bodies and arrows under the weight of history,
my obedient devices that will slip to a new home
like pilot fish even if I did live like a comic book,
my own kathump, a bonfire of small desires. Even
just seeing the old postman make it across the street,
overturning the itch to find another person disgusting:
two old ladies who sit nearby on a bench with great
white hair like surf, the way that a wave ends,
striking broken rocks. They hold small black purses,
open a mouth sometimes as if to speak, but cough
instead, the darkness growing, calling out to itself.

Eric the Swimmer

He was the first European. New in class,
dragging the wooden log of his accent,
stumbling over words but defiant
(while other boys swam and laughed)
with us few, standing in shallow water
to learn, trading looks, outmatched by larger
instructors who circled, slapped us with water
until we would try going under – the world

pulling up and smothering us, filling our ears.
My mind raced faster than the yellow
school bus each morning, our talks ended
in group faith: *I don't want to learn to swim.*

Then Eric honestly pleased, crying *I can swim!*
Breaking away, one stubborn General in war,
born again. And I changed too, flushing
over me, what I remember as a first betrayal.

I loved reactions, that I had spooned laughter
in air, and before all the lessons they asked me
if it was true Eric didn't know how to spell *the.*
But I didn't provide an answer, not wanting
to push buttons for that kind of laughter,
no – I don't think I gave an answer.

For All Undone Things

And they are many, loose as shoelaces
under our faces - inverted bowls with smiles
held underneath for a while, until lifted away.

My sister is pregnant, our mother gone
and she notes that our mother will never know
the child - leaving me to wonder
as her tear falls, if the thought of someone
gone could pass through someone who is,
and reach someone still forming, who hasn't
had a first taste of missing, of bitter milk -
what was that - you know it by now,

have heard it - scratchy as an old record player,
see it moving like the loose bolt
I would picture on amusement park rides.

Sun shows us our long shadows of the undone,
don't know why I rarely stop to laugh, a group
of people who chuckle like a strange engine,
how I turned away from a woman,
when all she wanted was. Listen, this is for you.

Try to wipe it all clean each night, thank God
for sleep, turn your eyes over and drop them
two stones into water. While you rest, the people
you know darken, a street of closed shops.

Instinct

Left Vancouver Island with the living blur
of a hummingbird in my head, having walked
over dried pine needles wary of cougars,
the hungry and desperate ones I read about.
Brochure cougars. Back at work, my hand twitches –
it already wants to stroke a keyboard again.
My voice is left in voicemail, a stone down a well.
Outside, trees form one line, like exhausted dancers.
Standing on a street corner at night I see a man
slowly painted in through thick fingers of darkness,
to arrive and stand with me, at the edge of my sight.

Looking at him, I find his head turns slowly over,
something lifeless caught in wind. Cannonball eyes
stare steadily from beneath a shore of grey hair.
The light changes and we both begin to step,
across the street, sailing back into lives that wait
on the corner. It's unexpected, a spider in a keyhole
venturing out onto my hand, the moment I realize
I need waves breaking, not a streetcar creaking,
and this waiting is slow suffocation. But it's too late,
the desire to kill that man just for looking at me
was my last bit of cougar hitting a glass wall.

Mama Spider

Mothers die and return as spiders, to stamp
every part of your home – the living room wall,
bathroom sink – with tenuous hope, defying
gravity to check on you in the days and months
after a funeral, they are found on shower curtains,
are knocked off and kicked down the drain, or
they try again and again just to get to you,
moving over shiny summer lawns, concrete
and guano, picked off by blackbirds, some
get as far as a window, self-hired in the humidity
to watch a while beneath cumulus and a sky
that's loaded with rain and eyeing the land.

For a moment that bacchanal, finally quiet man,
pear-shaped, asleep on a park bench, clinging
lightly to a book, comes near a truth on the swell
of a dream: remembers the lady in the shop
by the school, encouraging a banana over chocolate,
friendly to all the kids, her fan pushing back
at fat heat, humming like an old lighthouse.
She went into hospital for a too-big heart, and all
were smart enough to see the irony, but he'd dismiss
as drunkenness the idea of noble spiders, or her
nearly invisible in a room, relishing legs and legs,
the protein strands of silk, the secondary eyes.

The Echo of Isaac Brock

Still in uniform, but one of earth and tar:
coral epaulettes, strings of sand for hair,
a longtail for a screaming, out-of-focus hat.
Weary, but with discombobulated grin,
he passes with your annual epiphany,
learned to love French like one of his brothers.
He was between bonfires and church bells
on Confederation Day – allowed himself
to be hung with Riel, for the experience,
stowed away to stand with Billy Bishop
when he looked up at an azure sky to say
"Bet you don't get mud and horseshit
on you up there." Brock shook his head
over church-run schools meant to take
the Indian out of the Indians, the ban on
the sun dance, the potlatch, three Chinese
lives per mile of railway. His warm smile
grew into a laugh at the wind-slap of a subway
train arriving, and he thought "You and your
journey back and forth. It isn't that you
can't stay, it's that you don't know how to cling
to anything." His hands behind his back,
he walked in the snow with Trudeau.
He still slumbers in parts of the land,
a song and a bullet in his heart.

At Forty

He feels like a kid in a hardware store, half
his allowance spent, he needs to think
more carefully about the other half. Thinks
of the T. Rex, dead 65 million years but back
in a way it couldn't have conceived, the flat
and flickering climax of a film. He knows
he's the grunt that would've made a good general,
but never mind that now, at least it's no longer
a world with live cats burned in a wicker effigy.
He remembers standing in the heat of Florida
with his father, and when American singers beamed,
announced they were The Voices of Liberty,
his father said "I knew it," and turned away.
Trusts he's made of old moments that rattled
past like boxcars, has pain when typing, notes
the slow betrayal of his body, but senses
a much bigger pain behind other doors. And,
something new, his soul starting to get away,
trailing him for the first time, a red balloon.

Moving into History

From Oban we looked across confident water
to the toy cars and small homes, planted
like pins on the rolled moss of the Island.
Just below our bench where the tide

doesn't quite meet the shore, and birds
fight over nothing, the small trickle
of water in mud catches sunlight,
holds shivering diamonds.

And my hand only breaks the surface of
the ocean, trying to bring you this summer
day when we took pints of cool sea air
beneath the melting heat of the sun.

Iona showed us how it carved up sand
for long moments on the beach,
thin ribbons of water fingerpainting
paths and tiny cliff edges.

And at Castle Urquhart we looked over
walls worn down, could see from one
room into another. Above us, walking
back to town, the wild punctuation of crows.

Poem in the Sun

This poem appears in the sun – in the middle
of a great ball of burning hydrogen. Today
at lunch I sat outside and watched pigeons do
nothing. While the earth spins, they wander
and eat and shit everywhere that I want to sit.
The fly of the bird world. They've given up
on passion, but stand around all day long
with seagulls who haven't given up,
but don't know what they're screaming about.

But you're supposed to love your enemies,
so I break off some bread, throw it to a pigeon
while keeping a closer eye on myself. The bird
eats automatically, looks up at me with dead eyes
before walking away, and there is nothing
but a mud of contempt in me. So I wish
this page into the middle of the sun,
where Superman went once to burn himself clean,
and where it, mere paper, will be torched instantly.

Uncertain, Texas

There's a particular virtue, hidden in one level
of the dry wind, the idea that no one is sure
in this town of 151, or 154. There's a question,
somewhere on the halcyon surface of Caddo Lake,
where mooring was uncertain for steamboats,
and apocryphal men are shot down while swimming.

Nobody at the Uncertain flea market knows
why a loose cockatiel sits on a branch, steps out
from behind a curtain of Spanish moss with the idea
of doing more than nothing, steps back. Not flightless,
but it looks down to appear alarmed, wants the best
ephemeral stories, the lies with the most truth.

A boy runs back, up the concrete, filled-in footprints
of Socrates, says he saw Horseshoe crabs hustle slowly
up the beach, an invading pile of German helmets.
It's always something new with this boy. He's given
a lemonade, asked to relax. Before, he removed a bolt
that holds the universe together, said sorry about that.

Little Green Men

Frog-green bastards, gunk experts
half-buried under porches, or gripped
in sweaty hands. From some asylum
nation, binged on an esoteric set of morals –
it's all about handing out humility.
I'm sure I've bought a bag of bayonets,
machine-gunners, one radio man, a sniper,
a grenade thrower, a man waving *let's go*.
Patiently firecrackered officers of rage
and disgrace, they silently hum crooner
tunes to each other, have plastic dreams
of Germans to kill and women to slap
to swelling music, final days of obesity.
Me, I was all about a safe perimeter,
never wanted to invade, put a man
to scan the horizon. It's the one with
binoculars, the two-inch prick in my heart.

Basil Rathbone Meets God

God is a gold sphere covered in answers.
No, sapphire-bright and a bit of a pedant.
Wait, God is dinosaur-necked, standing
still to come forward and look him over.
It's weirdly as though he's onstage again
that kind of naked, can't-see-for-the-lights
feeling. He cycles through options: dastardly
villains, a black and white swashbuckler
with mango-coloured words, or the incisive
man he played in fourteen films, Sherlock.
In the second he ruminates, great men
are confused, blur like hot film burning
in the projector. There's a melee and Hitler
takes a stab at hustling out in the shape
of a giant squid, awesome eyes the size
of dinner plates – God sees it,
snaps him back, both of them yawning.
And there's Rathbone, with an apology,
his own equine body and features, a smile.

Tomorrow at Ten

I'll have a problem walking in. Beyond that,
I'm good, my heart a dull little apple learning
to swagger like an eggplant, just on the inside.
I'll be wavering on a street corner, caught
in someone else's tourist photo and framed
for a desk in Italy. Over there, the convenience
store has one toy, the Electronic Gorilla,
"Funny," but guaranteed to be bellicose again
and again, throw tiny chrome arms in the air.
What heart can it have, but one the size
of a peanut, reserved for toys and dictators?
A man starts each day descending to the basement,
stands a full minute with eyes closed, his back
to a wax Jack the Ripper. With this, each day
is a bonus. Heaven has too much sparkly shit
each time he pictures it. It's about being alive.
An explorer hollers into a squall, her placement
on a particular cliff-edge the product of one
slightly melted compass, one dented heart.
A Belgian man is in a coma twenty-three years,
conscious without anyone knowing, dreaming
his own comfortable jungle, the click-clack
of a stretcher, his favourite metal insect on the wall.
We are what we repeatedly do, Aristotle said.
And people have been saying it ever since.

For One Second at Midnight

You're in a doorway between houses, able to spot
the slurries that hold it all together, only able
to say *Um*, only now aware at this time the dead
tie a thin rope to everything, and pull. The second
has a particular grain, clear as crystal we might say,
if we thought to say it. For a second at midnight
anything is possible – you dated the cheerleader
or the quarterback, and pigeons know everything.
It's a window of opportunity, full
of luck, death and spirits – all superstitions are true
for a second, but few know that's the moment
to blow out your birthday cake, or throw salt over
the devil on your shoulder. As for me, for a second
I came close to inventing the device you wear over
your throat to call in sick and sound like hell, no need
to see office supplies at least one day. For a second
at midnight the world is like someone right in front
of you who stops walking, turns, laughing, lighting up,
but then gives a shit about getting out of your way.

Samuel Drowns, at Thirty

Samuel Drowns tapped the sleepy letters
of his name into place, made them hover
in the light of his computer screen before
he sent them away, and the screen folded
back and left, like a page turning.

Fragments of finished lives fought for place:
Samuel Drowns, Department of English
somewhere in the States, Captain Samuel Drowns
wrote about stripping and cleaning the FN rifle.
A Samuel Drowns sailed in 1801 from Ireland,
came in ninth in a 2002 bicycle race.
Samuel was president of the Irish Pistol Association
and the Samuel from a fishing vessel was lost at sea
off the coast of Nova Scotia, presumed dead.

This was too much, he turned his eyes away,
hating guns, the idea of being wiped from the deck
of a ship like a doll swept from a child's bed.
He lifted his body up and dropped it again
in front of the TV, turned it on for its screams.

I Just Have to Get Through This

Summer stayed no longer than a sparrow.
Medication is passed over a trembling lip.
The postcard arrives one day too late.
A man notes he'll get an Asian hooker if
he's dying, maybe if he isn't. A spider
in the woodpile ends up in the fire.
One beggar spits in the air at another.
The field of sunflowers holds on as long
as it can, but dies before the gentle old lady
passes on the train. Babies are placed
in planes and carried to cars. A good man
is murdered in his house. They leave
his body, pass his son on the lawn, reach
out to ruffle his hair, and he watches them go.

For some reason we all wait for something.

Orwell Robot

He's an epicurean droid, self-maintaining,
solar-peppered, laugh like a cotton machine gun
and he's all that's left, the only man after
our best war, his little tin spine better-lasting.
A thousand years old, fed with every word,
he leaves Orwell comments on the air here,
and there, wheels around to a tidy mania
of things he collected and stacked, smokes,
calls himself Kafkaesque, and laughs, stops
to balk at fading red prices posted on a corner.
All that's left of the best of us, he seizes a daft
mademoiselle mannequin by the lumbar, and
if it doesn't go into the fissure for plastic,
to land next to some cowboy (alarmed, the time
he chucked a persimmon into the pit) he simply
stacks her with the others, thinking there you go
with your googly eyes, now you have company.
He allows himself a minute a day to dream
of liftoff, look at the sky, remember the Spanish
soldier now centuries dead, the one with the open,
beaming face that marched off into the sun.

A Stuntman Destroys the Hate Window

Astute in subtle ways, it's a bitter fence of chipped
white paint, toothless at times, no kind of struggle
to get in. The house watched its cheerful boys go out
to die in war, daughters choose the wrong small-town
man to marry, all from a solitary perch on the hill.
It's a little subliminal, the window where the hate
pooled, subjective glass of deep memes, a black frame
of patchwork pattern, pieces stained red and yellow.
The location scout tests each dry porch board slowly
as they all sigh *fine, fine,* reaches the window to stand
hands in pockets, declare out loud the glass makes you
squint to see through, damn strange constipated glass.
He hates every motherfucking deviant bastard down
below in the town, but is alone, nobody is right outside
and it's a boneless kind of anger. He pulls free.
House bought, hope lies in a small film crew – nobody
out there as someone looks through – and a stuntman,
one man with a muscle fetish, who says *fucking*
ugly window as cameras roll, takes a running leap,
and his inertia does the rest. For a symbiotic second
he's one with the glass, which feels thin but strong
before it shatters into a bled-out constellation
over padding and grass. The following morning,
the stuntman sits next to the director, crosses a leg,
lights a smoke, says *seems a little brighter doesn't it.*

No One on the Streetcar

No one on the streetcar can explain
who picks up the two halves of the street
and pushes them along as we sit.
Someone holds a newborn delicately
as a candle, an old woman coughs regularly,
interrupting talk like a church organ.
No one knows who can possibly pay enough
to have all the unsaid swept up,
what collects around our feet like litter.
No one stops to think that placed here,
our small lives sit like eggs in a carton.
No one realizes time travel is easy,
we'll arrive at our future, no matter what,
No one heard I said goodbye to a woman
yesterday for the last time, stood and watched
her board a bus, and let her go.
I came out on the other side, she'd later say.
No one else spotted the dead spider
I found this morning in my apartment,
hung by its own ideas between my boots.

Swallowed

The woman orders coffee and knows.
And some kind of sticky bun, moments
sneaking over like clouds. Thank you
and stepping over the seconds to a table.
Seating herself. Forty. Unwrapping a scarf.
Happy alone, more likely just all right.

Or does she know, scratch the paint on days,
look through that man now at the counter
saying two.. two.. pieces of cake,
holding two fingers flat in air as if he plans
to poke the owner in the eyes.
Underneath her how time burst, a match

into a pool of gas, the days like an army
of soldiers pulling themselves from trenches,
running into gunfire, falling one at a time.
How we speak to walls of air, how forgetting
is as simple as light snow over railway tracks.
I see her, she reaches for her coffee first.

Acknowledgements

Some of these poems appeared in *Taddle Creek, Misunderstandings Magazine, Wonk, The Toronto Quarterly* and *Nthposition*.

I'm grateful for financial support from the Ontario Arts Council.

The poem "The Least Important Man" was inspired by an online reference to a story of the same name by Steven Moffat.

"Uncertain, Texas" was inspired by several musician friends of mine visiting the town.

Many thanks to Dan Wells, Eric Ormsby, Tara Murphy and everyone at Biblioasis, for producing this book and all the remarkable work they're doing.

Thank you to all these friends: Nada Ashkar, Kahn Nomura, Sue Heal, Sandra Nakata, Arlynn MacDermott, Shereen Chang.

This book is dedicated to my mother, Margaret Joan Boyd, who'd have said there's no such thing as a least important person.

About The Author

Alex Boyd writes poems, fiction, reviews and essays. His work appears in publications such as *The Globe and Mail*, *Quill & Quire*, and on *Nthposition*. His first book of poems, *Making Bones Walk* (Luna Publications, 2007) won the Gerald Lampert Award. He edits the online poetry journal *Northern Poetry Review*, and recently helped establish *Best Canadian Essays*, co-editing the first two editions of selections from Canadian magazines.